ILLUSTRATED BY JAZMIN MENCIA

Dedication

This book is dedicated to my four children:
Khayleb, Baby Boy, Brielle, and Cameron,
who by their very presence in my life,
push my creativity to higher places.

Love you always 💛

This Book Belongs To

....

....

Hi! I'm Henry. I have lots of friends.
Friends are kind. Friends make us happy.
We do not bite our friends.
Biting hurts.
Biting stings.
Biting friends is not a nice thing.

Friends are cool. Friends can play.
Friends can chase outside all day.
We do not bite our friends.
Biting hurts.
Biting stings.
Biting friends is not a nice thing.

Friends can splish. Friends can splash.
Friends can do a happy dash.
We do not bite our friends.
Biting hurts.
Biting stings.
Biting friends is not a nice thing.

Friends are fun. Friends are great.
Friends can help you celebrate.
We do not bite our friends.
Biting hurts.
Biting stings.
Biting friends is not a nice thing.

Friends can hug. Friends can share.
Friends can give a lot of care.
We do not bite our friends.
Biting hurts.
Biting stings.
Biting friends is not a nice thing.

Friends can skip. Friends can run.
Friends can have lots of fun.
We do not bite our friends.
Biting hurts.
Biting stings.
Biting friends is not a nice thing.

Note to Parents:

Why do babies and toddlers bite?

Babies and toddlers bite for a multitude of reasons.
Whether they are teething, seeking oral input, or in need
of attention, biting is common.

Babies and toddlers lack the verbal communication skills
required to effectively communicate their frustrations,
anger, and fears. Biting is often a way of expressing these
feelings.

How to prevent biting?

Pay attention to your child during play. Consider the
following:
What happened before the biting occurred?
Who did your child bite?
Where was your child?

If you see signs of behavior that may
lead to biting:

Distract your child with a toy
(perhaps something they haven't played with in a while).

Take time to talk to your child about how to resolve the issue.

Engage your child in reading a book. Books about sharing,
feelings, or biting can be helpful.

Resources parents may find helpful

Talk to your child about different feelings and situations that may result in biting.

Happy

Surprised

Silly

Scared

Sad

Angry

Talk to your child about things that are appropriate to put in their mouth.

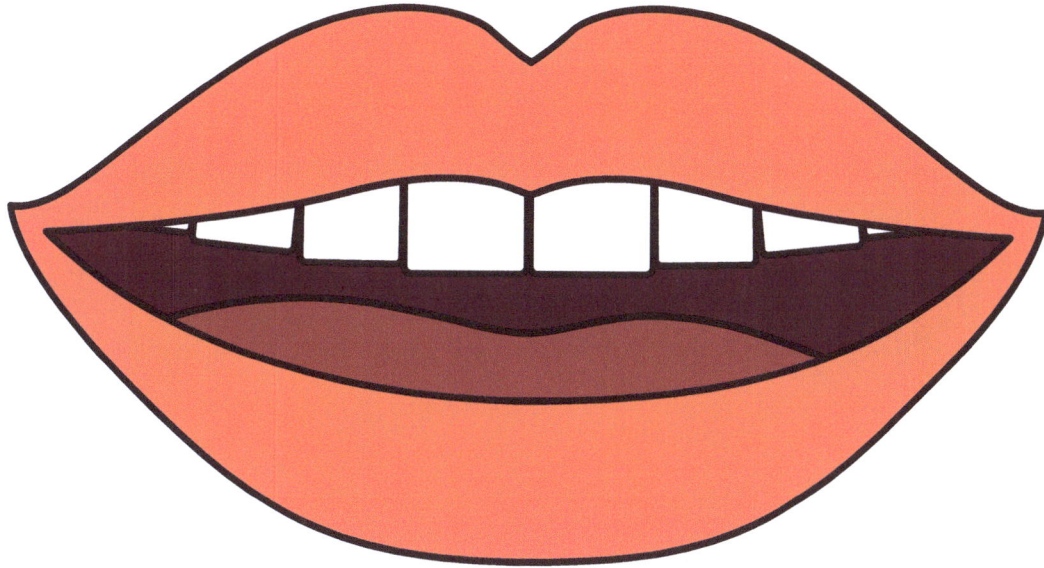

Fruits

Veggies

Treats

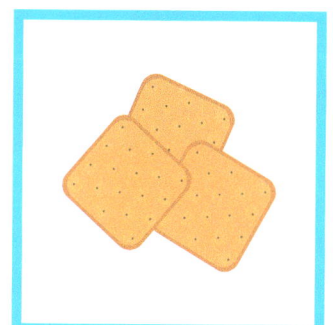

Crackers

Talk to your child about things that are not appropriate to put in their mouth.

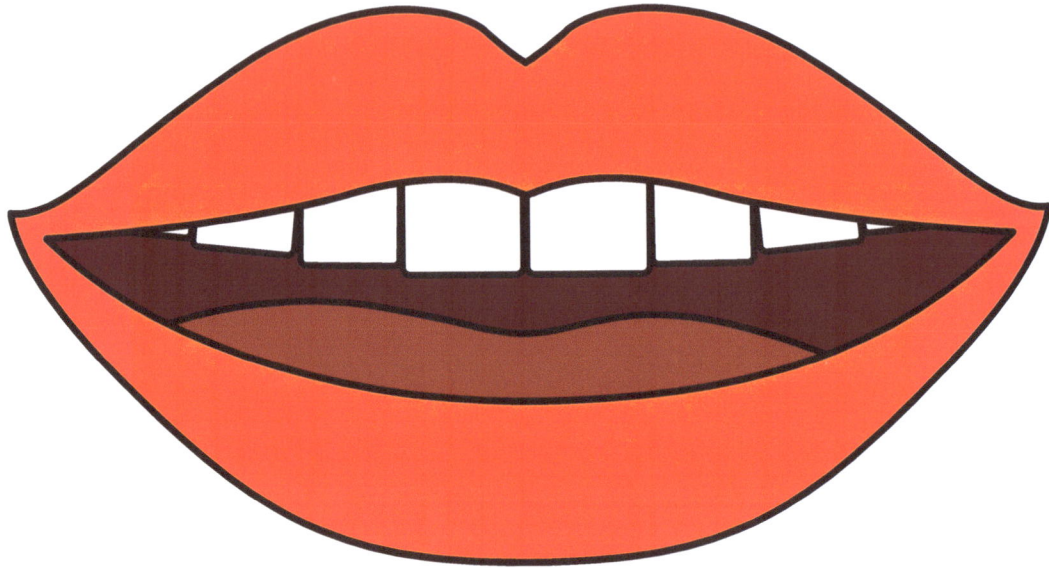

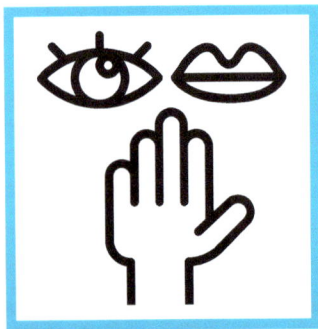

Other people's body parts

Trash

Hand Sanitizer

Clothing

Talk to your child about other things they can do with friends.

Toss a ball

**Play in
the park**

Jump

Give a high five for being a good friend.
Praise your child whenever they are caught
sharing, taking turns, or playing nicely
with their friends. This reinforces positive behavior.

Note to Parents:

Love on your child, but don't forget to love on yourself. Parenting is challenging.

www.ingramcontent.com/pod-product-compliance
Lightning Source LLC
Chambersburg PA
CBHW042113040426
42448CB00002B/261